YOUNG SCIENTISTS INVESTIGATE

Light and Colour

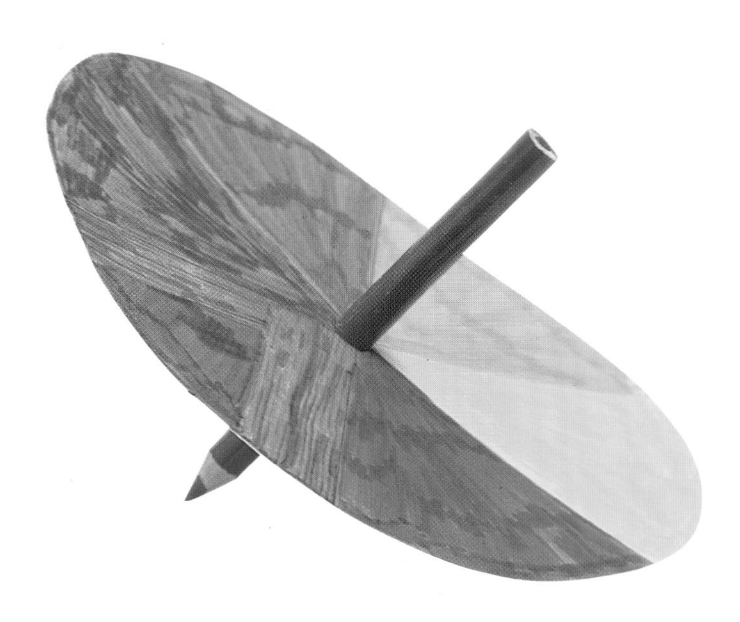

Malcolm Dixon
and Karen Smith

Evans Brothers Limited

NOTES FOR TEACHERS AND PARENTS

What is light? (pages 6-7)
The children should be encouraged to talk about and list, as sources of light, the following — the sun, stars, the moon (reflects light), electric lights including street lights, gas fires, lightning, candles, fireworks and television screens. Remind the children of the dangers of electricity, gas fires, candles and, especially, that they should never look directly at the sun.

Shadows (pages 8-9)
The children need to go into the playground and investigate shadows for themselves. Indoors, let the children use their hands to make animal shapes and cast shadows. Give the children a torch and some materials — some transparent and some opaque — and let them investigate which cast shadows and which do not. Talk about the differences between the materials.

What is dark? (pages 10-11)
It would be helpful to use a torch (the sun) and a globe (the earth) to show how day and night are created. The practical activity with the darkroom shows that nothing can be seen without light. The torch emits light and the shiny objects reflect light. The black paper reflects very little light. Try this activity with a white-lined box and notice the difference in the amount of light reflected.

Light travels (pages 12-13)
Remind the children not to look directly at the sun because it can damage their eyes. Discuss the way in which light travels in **all** directions from the bulb. When they move or bend their tubes the light from the bulb is unable to travel to their eyes. Playing with torches, in darkened rooms, will help to develop the idea of light travelling in straight lines.

Reflections (pages 14-15)
Flat, shiny surfaces such as mirrors produce images of whatever is in front of them. Mirrors reverse images — the left side appears to be the right.

Curved mirrors (pages 16-17)
When a child looks in the front of a spoon (a concave mirror) they will see a small inverted image. The back of a spoon (convex mirror) produces a small image the right way up.

Rainbow colours (pages 18-19)
Children find the activity, using a prism, very exciting. The patch of coloured light is called a spectrum. The prism acts like raindrops in producing a rainbow.

Colours around us (pages 20-21)
When children are attempting these tasks be sensitive to those children (one in eight boys) who may have difficulties because they are colour-blind.

Changing colours (pages 22-23)
Let the children experience these colour changes for themselves, if possible contrasting them with coloured lights (page 27). Red, yellow and blue paint make dark brown. (page 23) This shows that these inks are made up of a number of different colours.

Camouflage (pages 24-25)
Try to show the children photographs of chameleons which can change their colour to match their surroundings. Talk about camouflage when visiting a zoo. Try to provide a variety of materials for the children to use when making their camouflage box. A shoe box is, in fact, a reasonable size for this activity.

Mixing light (pages 26-27)
If possible use three torches and coloured filters (from a photographic shop) — red, blue and green — and allow the children to investigate the lights mixing. When the disc spins quickly our eyes are unable to see the separate colours. We see the different coloured light mixed together. It appears greyish-white. Notice that mixing light colours is different from mixing paint colours (see page 23).

Light for growth (pages 28-29)
If possible visit a greenhouse and talk about the light travelling through the glass.The practical activity will provide an opportunity to talk about a 'fair test' and show the importance of light in plant growth. Place one of the trays in a light, but not too sunny place. To test if grass grows towards light you might use a box with a hole in one side. The grass, inside the box, will grow towards the hole and the light!

YOUNG SCIENTISTS INVESTIGATE

Light and Colour

This edition first published in 2005 by
Evans Brothers Limited
2A Portman Mansions
Chiltern St
London W1U 6NR

ISBN 0 237 53019 8

British Library Cataloguing in Publication Data
A catalogue record for this book is available from the British Library.

Acknowledgements
Editorial: Su Swallow
Design: Neil Sayer/Rob Walster
Production: Jenny Mulvanny
Commissioned photography: Alan Towse

The publishers would like to thank Mr Rowlings, the staff, parents and children of Halsnead C.P School and the children of Belvedere Junior School for their help in the preparation of this book. We would also like to thank the children of Woolton Infant School who appear on the cover of this book.

For permission to reproduce copyright material the authors and publishers gratefully acknowledge the following:
Page 6 Alan Towse **page 10** Robert Harding Picture Library **page 12** Jon Delorme/Robert Harding Picture Library **page 16** John Hulme/Eye Ubiquitous **page 18** Nick Servian/Robert Harding Picture Library **page 20** Adam Woolfit/Robert Harding Picture Library **page 21** H.P. Merten/Robert Harding Picture Library **page 24** Gerald Hoberman/Robert Harding Picture Library **page 26** Colin Willoughby/Performing Arts Library **page 28** Gerard Lacz/NHPA

Contents

What is light?

Your eyes need light to see. Without light you would have to rely on your senses of hearing, touch, smell and taste.
Green plants need sunlight to grow and make food for us and other animals.

We get most of our light from the sun.
We also make our own light to use in our homes and schools and in the streets.
Why do we need to make our own light?

REMEMBER – NEVER LOOK STRAIGHT AT THE SUN. IT CAN DAMAGE YOUR EYES

Work with a friend

Where does light come from?

Talk with your friends about the things that give us light.
Make a list of all the things you can think of.
Draw some of these things.

You will need:
pencil
coloured pencils or crayons
paper
magazines
scissors

Find out more!
Look through some magazines and cut out pictures of things that give out light.

Shadows

The children in the photograph are standing with their backs to the sun. Light from the sun is shining on them but it cannot go through their bodies. Look at their shadows on the ground.
Will the children be able to stand on their shadows?
Will their shadows move when they move?
How could you investigate this?

Make shadows

Draw a figure on some card.
Cut around the edge.
Use paints to make the figure look attractive.
When the paints have dried fix a length of wood to the back of the card.
Hold your figure so that the sun shines on it. If there is no sunshine use a torch in a dark room.
Look at the shadow.

You will need:

card
paints
scissors
lengths of wood such as dowel
glue or sticky tape
torch

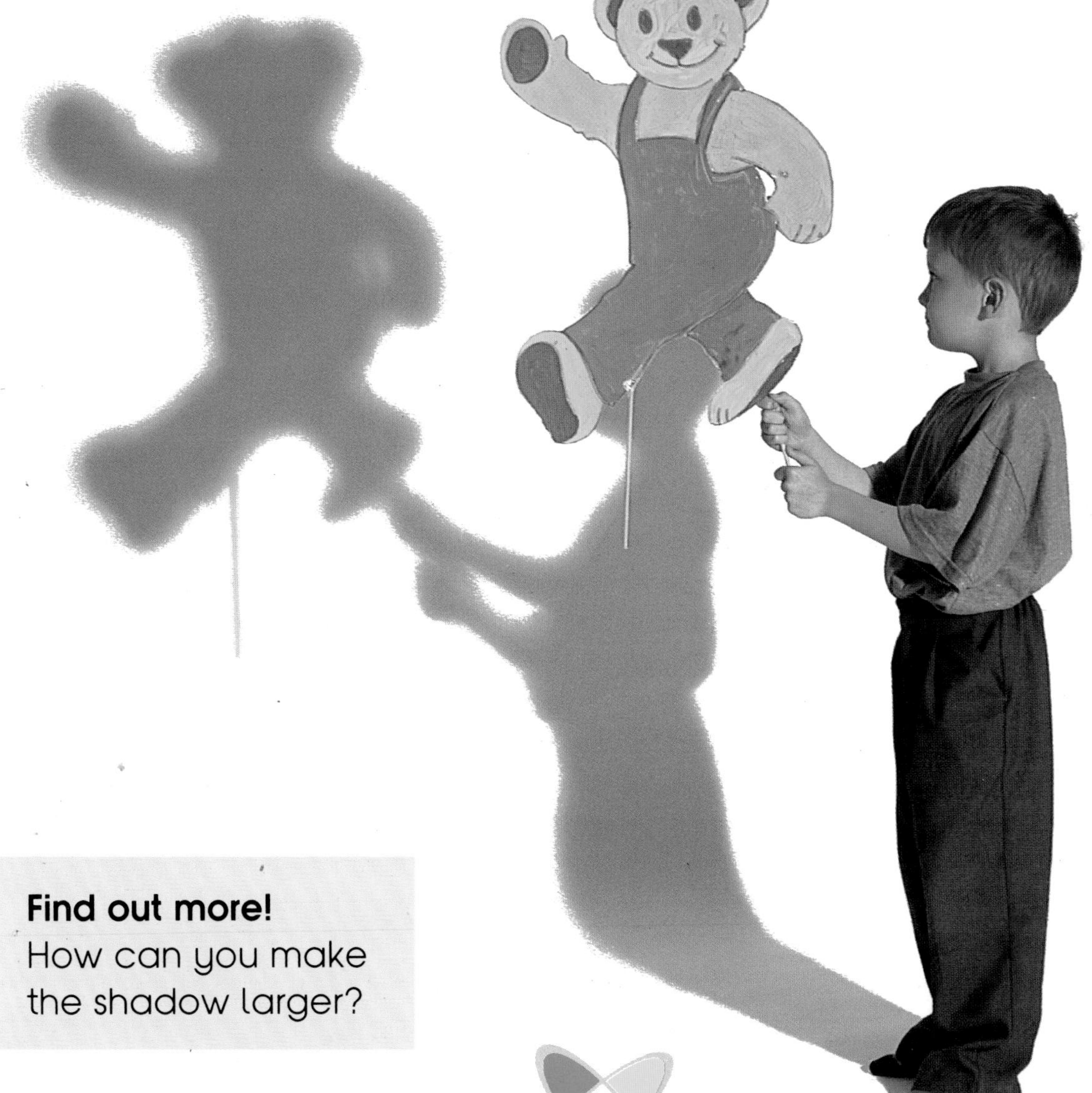

Find out more!
How can you make the shadow larger?

What is dark?

Part of each day is light and part is dark. Our planet, the earth, turns round and round. When the part of the earth where you are faces the sun then there is light. We say it is daytime. When your part of the earth turns away from the sun it starts to go dark. We call this night-time.
During the night we need our own lights. Look at the photograph. You can see that the sky is dark and the buildings and bridge are lit up.

Make a darkroom

Cover the inside of the box, and the lid, with black paper.
Make a small hole in the side of the box.
Put the lid on the box. Look through the hole.
What can you see inside your darkroom?
Put some shiny objects inside your darkroom.
Replace the lid and look through the hole.
What can you see?
Switch on the torch and place it in the darkroom.
Can you see anything? Can you explain why?

You will need:

large box
black paper
glue
scissors
torch
aluminium foil
shiny objects

Light travels

Look at this photograph. You can see rays of sunlight shining through the trees. Light travels in straight lines. It moves very quickly at a fantastic speed of 300,000 kilometres per second. Scientists believe nothing can travel faster than light. Even so, it takes eight minutes for light from the sun, which is 150 million kilometres away, to reach us.

Work with some friends

How does light travel?

Screw the bulb into the bulb-holder.
Use the wires and crocodile clips to connect the battery to the bulb-holder.
The bulb should light up.
Give some cardboard tubes to some of your friends. Make the room dark.
Ask them to look at the bulb light through their tubes.
You can see, from the position of the tubes, that light travels in straight lines from the bulb to your friends' eyes.

You will need:
cardboard tubes
battery
bulb in bulb-holder
4 crocodile clips
two covered wires

Find out more!
What happens when your friends move or bend their tubes?

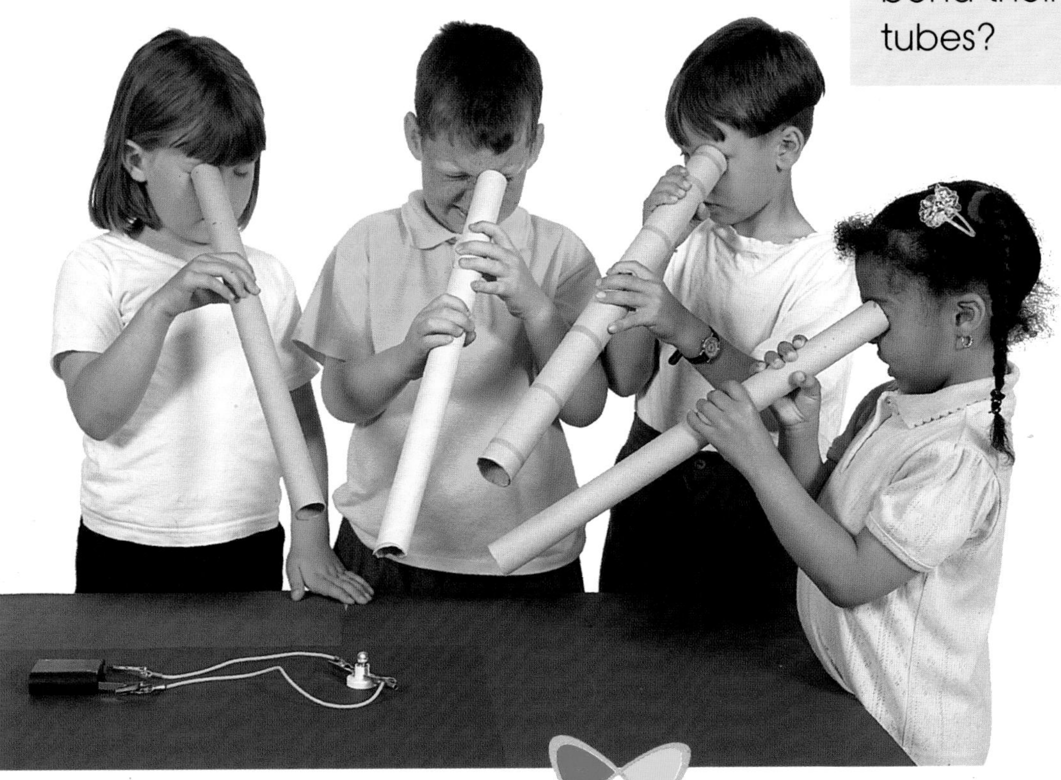

Reflections

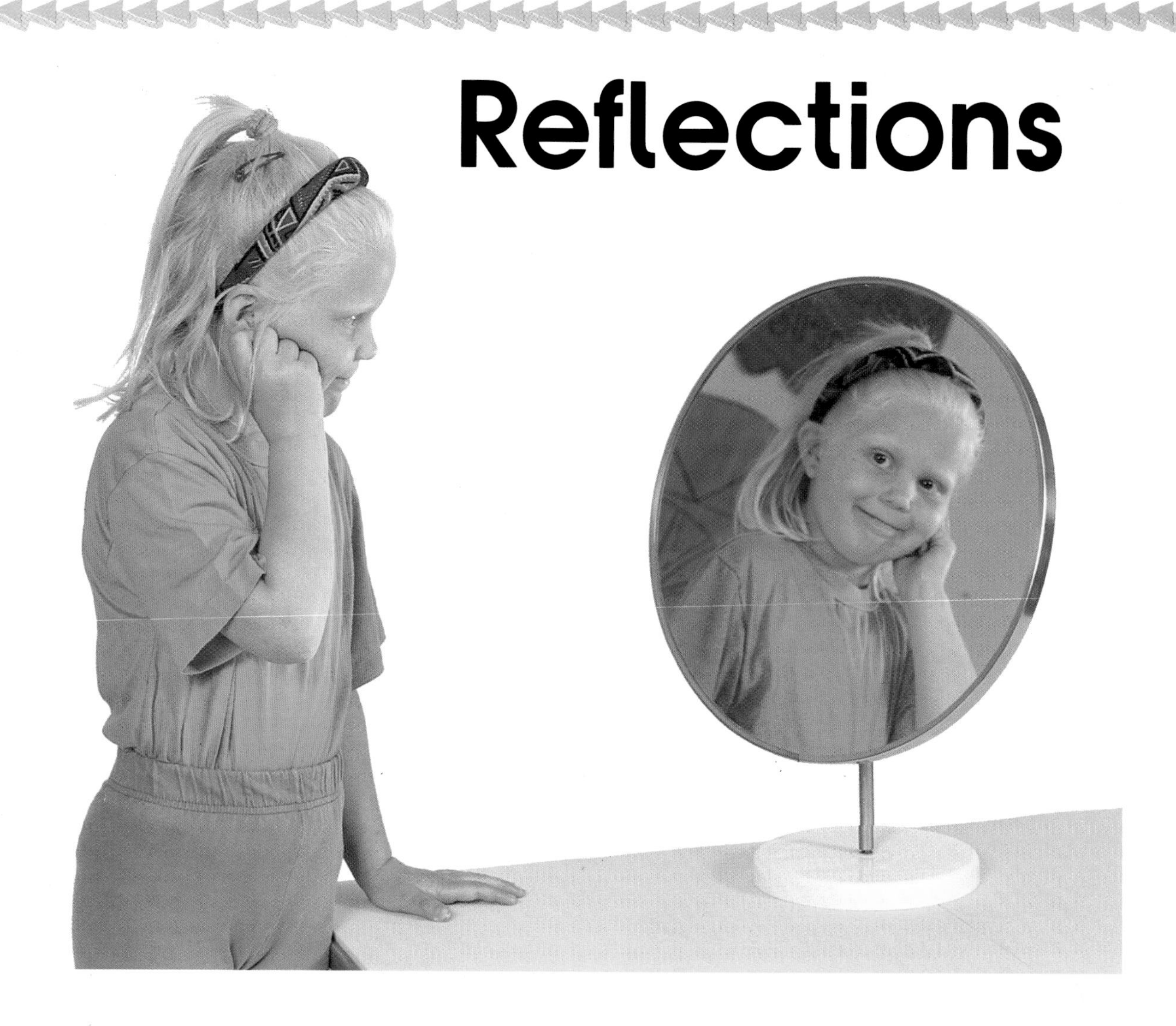

Much of the light that falls on things 'bounces off' again. Scientists say it is reflected. Shiny surfaces, such as mirrors, reflect light the best. The girl in the photograph is looking at her reflection in a mirror. She is touching her face with her right hand.
Look at her image in the mirror.
Which hand is touching her face in the mirror?
Does this always happen when someone looks in a mirror? Try it yourself.

How many images can you see?

Tape the edges of two mirrors together.
Stand the mirrors on a table.
Place your small toy between the mirrors.
How many images can you see?

You will need:
two flat plastic mirrors
sticky tape
small toy

Find out more!
Move the mirrors closer together.
How many images can you see now?
What happens when you move them even closer together?

Curved mirrors

The images made by curved mirrors are different from those in flat mirrors.
They can change the shape and size of the things relected in them.
Have you ever looked at yourself in a large curved mirror?

Have fun with curved mirrors

You will need:
flexible mirror card
large spoons
polished ornaments
polished pans and kettles

Look at your face in each side of a shiny spoon.
What do you see?
Bend the mirror card.
Look at your image in the curved surface.
Bend the mirror the other way.
Does this make any difference to your image ?
Look at your image in other curved and polished surfaces.

Rainbow colours

Sunlight appears to be colourless. It is called 'white light' but it is really made up of different colours. You can see these colours when a rainbow appears in the sky. This happens when the sun shines while it is still raining. These colours — red, orange, yellow, green, blue, indigo and violet — are called the spectrum.

Make your own rainbow

You will need:
plastic prism (if unavailable use an empty clear plastic ballpoint pen case)

On a very sunny day hold the prism in the sunlight.
Turn the prism slowly so that light goes through it.
Try to keep your fingers out of the way!
Look out for a patch of coloured light on the ground or wall, or use white paper.
What colours can you see? Check these colours with the rainbow colours on the opposite page.

 **REMEMBER – DON'T LOOK STRAIGHT AT THE SUN**

Colours around us

We have colours all around us. Our skins are different colours and we wear different coloured clothes. Look at all the colours in this photograph. What colours are the buildings? What colour clothing are the people wearing? What would life be like without colour?

How does colour help you?

You will need:
paper
pencil

Each country of the world has its own flag. Flags have bright colours and bold patterns. Do you know any of the flags in the photograph?

Talk with some friends about how colour helps you. Draw some of the ways you think of.

Changing colours

When you are painting you can mix the paints and make a new colour. If you mix red paint and yellow paint it makes orange. Blue and yellow make green. Blue and red make purple.
Red, yellow and blue are the primary colours of paint. You can use them to make any other colour. What happens when you mix red, yellow and blue paint together?

Investigate colours

Ask an adult to help you draw and cut out some butterfly shapes. Decorate one butterfly shape with dots using a black felt-tip pen. Use a straw to drop water on to the dots. What happens to the dots? What colours can you see?

Find out more!
Use other colours to decorate some of the other butterflies.
What happens when you drop water on to these colours?
What does this tell you about the colours of felt-tip pens?

You will need:

blotting or filter paper
different coloured felt-tip pens
scissors
plastic containers filled with water
straws

Camouflage

Some animals have colours and patterns that match their surroundings. This helps them to stay hidden. It is called camouflage.
Look at the tiger in this photograph. The stripes on its body help it to blend into tall grass. This helps it to creep up on its prey and stay hidden until it is ready to pounce.
Can you think of other animals that camouflage themselves?

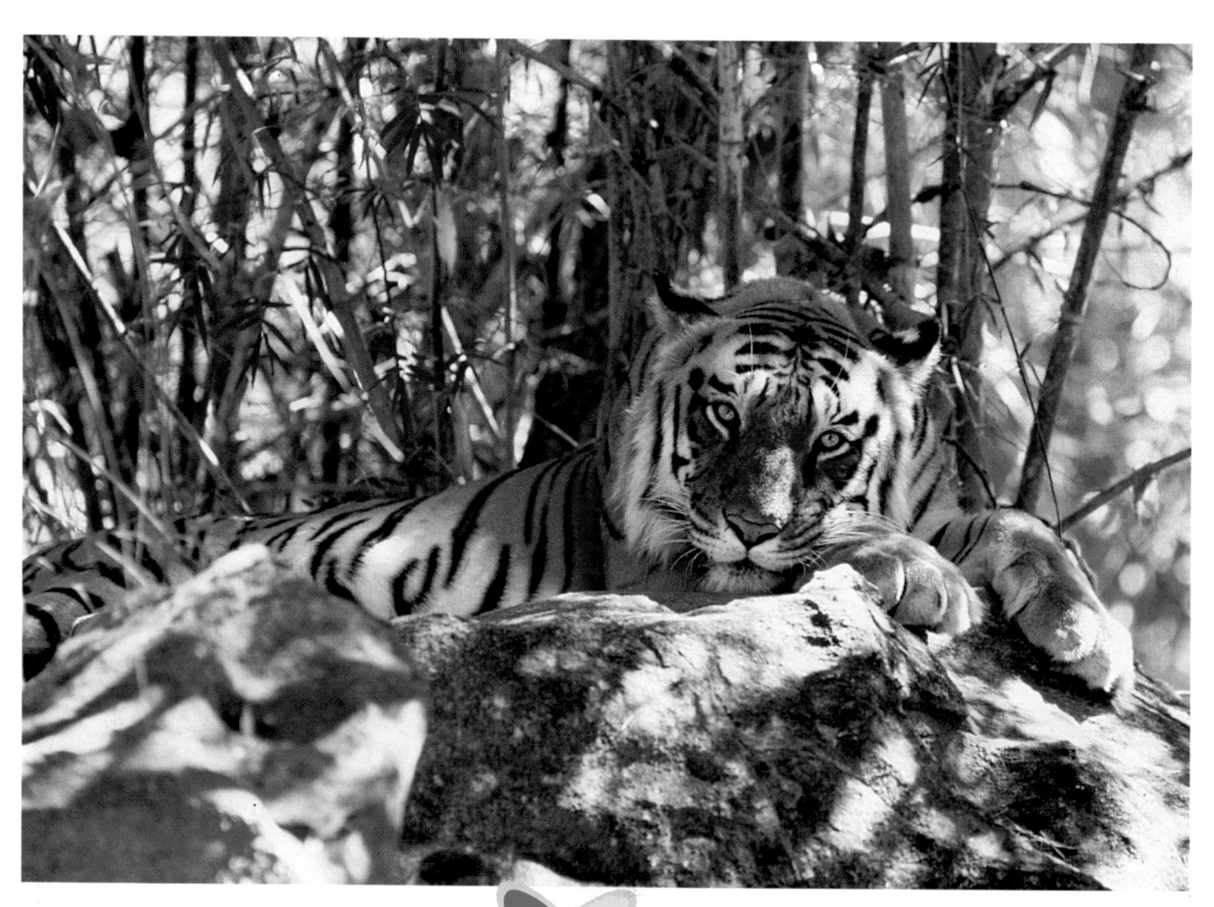

Investigate camouflage

Look in some books at photographs of tigers. Ask an adult to help you draw one. Use paints or coloured pencils to colour in your drawing.
Now think of how you can make a home, in the box, for your tiger. You can use paints, straw and other materials. Look at your tiger in its home.
How well is it camouflaged?

You will need:

large box
card
paints
coloured pencils
scissors
straw

Mixing light

Coloured light can be mixed. You may have seen this at a theatre, perhaps when watching a show or pantomime, when lights are used to create different effects. You can see theatre lights in the photograph.
Red, blue and green are known as the primary colours of light. When red and green lights are mixed they make yellow. When red, blue and green are mixed they make white.

Show that white light is a mixture of colours

Place the plate on the white card.
Draw around it. Cut out the circle.
Use a ruler to help you draw six sections on the card.
Colour each section a colour of the rainbow.
Push a pencil through the card.
Spin your coloured card.
What colour is it when spinning fast?

You will need:
white card
scissors
coloured pencils or crayons
ruler
plastic or paper plate

Find out more!
Make other spinners.
Colour them in different patterns.
What happens when you spin them fast?

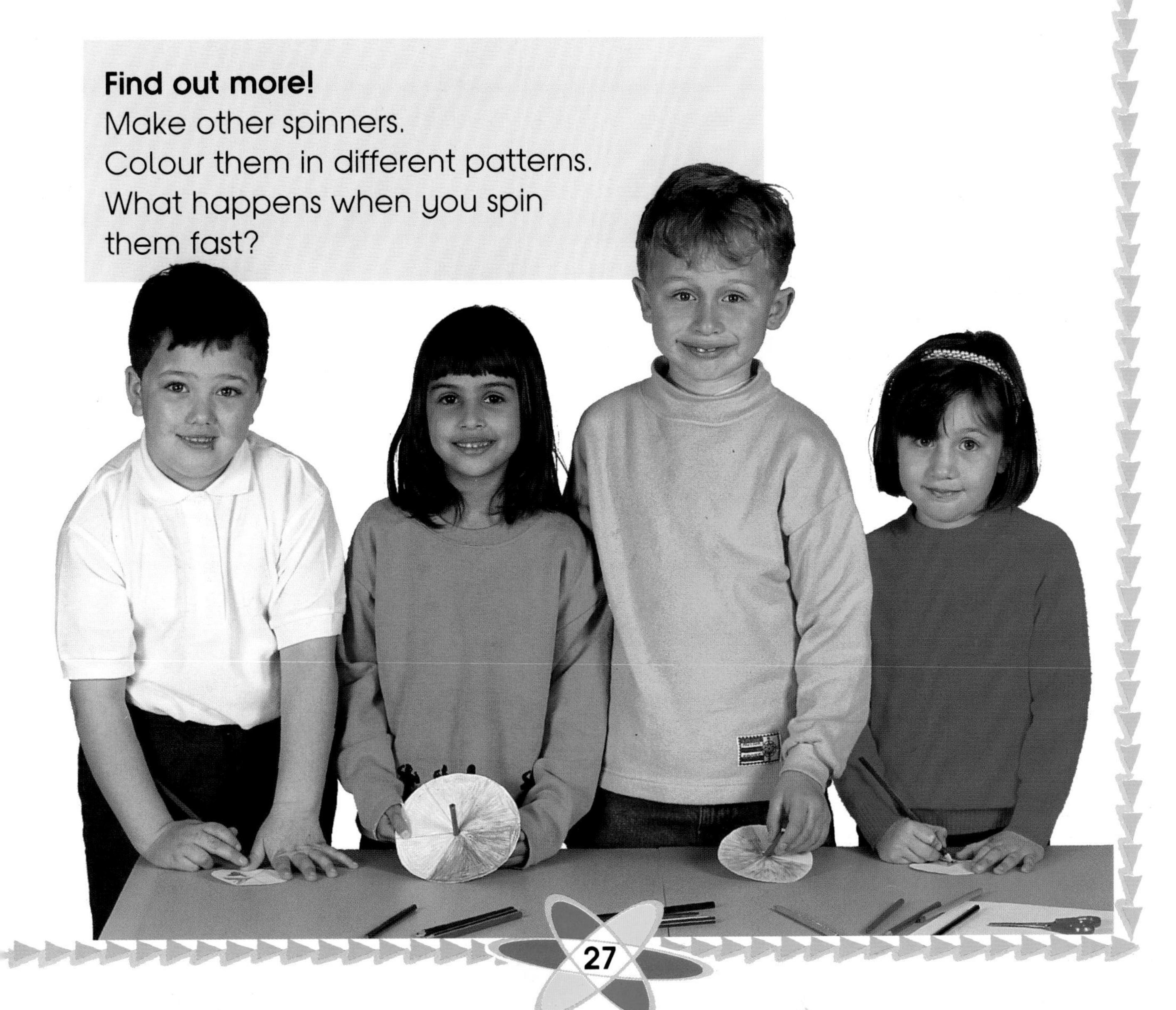

Light for growth

Plants need light to grow. If light is all around them the plants will grow straight up. If not, they bend and grow towards the light. Look at the photograph of sunflowers. All the flowers are facing the sun. Look in your garden, too. Can you see any plants that are bending towards the light? Do you have a greenhouse? Light and heat from the sun travel through the glass and help the plants to grow faster.

Watch some seeds grow

Soak the paper towels in water and place one in each tray.
Sprinkle some grass seeds on to each of the wet towels.
Place each tray into a polythene bag.
Make a 'greenhouse' for the seeds by blowing into the bags. Tie the ends to keep the bags inflated. Place one bag in a very dark cupboard. Place the other seeds in a light place.
Look at the seeds every day.
Do you notice any differences? Why do you think this happens?

You will need:
two small polystyrene trays
two paper towels
grass seeds
two clear polythene bags

Find out more!
Think of a way to test if grass seeds grow towards the light.

Index